Lunar Odyssey:
The Scientific Wonders of Apollo 11
Technology

Marc Ferrari X

"That's one small step for man, one giant leap for mankind."

Neil Armstrong

TABLE OF CONTENTS

PART I: Prelude to Exploration

Chapter 1: The Space Race and Apollo 11's Genesis

Hey there, fellow space enthusiasts! Can you imagine a time when Earth's most powerful nations were locked in a friendly (well, not so friendly) competition to see who could conquer the cosmos first? That's the thrilling backdrop of the Space Race, a period that paved the way for the incredible achievement of Apollo 11's lunar landing. So, grab your helmets and buckle up for a journey into the heart of this technological adventure!

The Political and Ideological Landscape: Catalyst for Exploration

Back in the mid-20th century, the world was split between two major powerhouses: the United States and the Soviet Union. It wasn't just about who had the bigger military toys; it was also about ideologies, beliefs, and, of course, science. The launch of the Soviet satellite Sputnik 1 in 1957, that little metal ball orbiting Earth, triggered a collective jaw-drop globally. The world realised that the heavens were suddenly accessible, and the Space Race kicked off in earnest.

The Mercury and Gemini Programs: Stepping Stones to Apollo

In the U.S., NASA became the hero we didn't know we needed. They kicked off with the Mercury program, aiming to send brave astronauts into the great beyond. They succeeded, with Alan Shepard making a quick trip in 1961. But NASA wasn't satisfied with just orbiting Earth; they aimed higher. The Gemini program took the baton, teaching astronauts how to spacewalk, work in orbit, and, importantly, dock spacecraft together. These programs were like training wheels for the grandest ride yet: Apollo 11.

Kennedy's Moonshot Challenge: A Nation's Determination

Picture this: It's 1961, and President John F. Kennedy stands before a crowd, including some skeptical eyebrows. He drops a bombshell: "Let's land a human on the Moon and bring them back home safely... before this decade ends!" Cue the raised eyebrows turning into jaws hitting the floor. This bold challenge wasn't just a political move; it was a beacon of human achievement that rallied an entire nation. The clock started ticking, and the Apollo program was off and running.

Technological Visionaries: Architects of Apollo 11

Behind every extraordinary feat, there are extraordinary people. In the case of Apollo 11, we had some real visionaries leading the charge. Take Wernher von Braun, for instance. This German engineer wasn't just any rocket scientist; he played a starring role in crafting the Saturn V rocket, the colossal beast that would carry humans to the Moon. And then there's John Houbolt, who championed the lunar orbit rendezvous method - a brilliant plan that saved time, fuel, and brainpower.

Technological Challenges on the Horizon

Apollo 11 wasn't just a casual Sunday stroll. It was more like a cosmic puzzle with thousands of pieces. Think about it: creating life support systems for astronauts in the harsh vacuum of space, developing communication equipment that could transmit messages across unthinkable distances, and designing a spacecraft that could gracefully land on the Moon and make it back home in one piece. It's like solving a Rubik's Cube on steroids!

A Foundation for Exploration

As the Apollo program gained traction, so did our collective know-how. The technological marvels born from this era weren't just for space; they sparked revolutions in computing, materials science, and more. When Apollo 11 triumphantly touched down on the lunar surface, it wasn't just a win for the U.S.; it was a testament to what humans can achieve when we dream big, work together, and challenge ourselves. The Space Race wasn't just a race; it was an invitation to explore the unknown, powered by the innovation that defines us as a species.

Chapter 2: The Lunar Dream: Early Concepts and Challenges

Hey there, fellow cosmic adventurers! Buckle up, because in this chapter, we're diving deep into the early days of lunar exploration. Picture a time when the Moon was a distant, tantalising dream, and space travel was more science fiction than science fact. From whimsical space mirrors to seeds destined for lunar soil, let's unravel the intriguing tale of how we went from gazing at the Moon to aiming for its surface.

Dreaming Beyond the Sky: The Birth of Lunar Exploration

Back in the late 1800s, the skies were abuzz with the imagination of pioneers like Jules Verne. These storytellers weaved tales of brave souls embarking on journeys to the Moon, capturing the hearts and minds of those who gazed up at the night sky. However, the idea of actually stepping foot on the lunar surface was almost as fantastical as the stories themselves. But as history has shown, human imagination knows no bounds.

Early Ideas: Rockets, Canons, and Crazy Schemes

As the 20th century dawned, the seeds of space travel were sown by brilliant minds like Konstantin Tsiolkovsky and Robert Goddard. These visionaries dared to dream of rockets as more than mere fireworks —they saw them as vehicles to propel us beyond Earth's boundaries. Yet, their early rocket designs were met with raised eyebrows. After all, convincing people that we could journey to the Moon by riding atop explosive propulsion wasn't exactly a walk in the park!

The Space Mirror and Other Outlandish Ideas

Hold onto your hats, because this is where things get really creative! In the 1920s, Yuri Kondratyuk tossed out the idea of a "space mirror," a fantastical device that would focus sunlight onto a spaceship's sail, pushing it towards the Moon. It sounds like something straight out of a steampunk novel, doesn't it? Meanwhile, on the other side of the world, Robert H. Goddard proposed a plan to send a rocket to the Moon with seeds on board, hoping lunar plants would thrive. While these ideas might seem far-fetched now, they reveal the wild lengths to which people were willing to go for a chance at lunar exploration.

The Call of Sputnik: A New Era Dawns

Ah, 1957—cue the dramatic music! The world was introduced to a new era with a beeping metal sphere: Sputnik 1. The Soviet Union had managed to hurl the first-ever artificial satellite into orbit. This momentous event not only kicked off the grand Space Race but also reignited the collective fascination with the Moon. Suddenly, our closest cosmic neighbour went from a distant curiosity to a tangible destination—a place that humans might actually set foot upon.

The Hurdles: Gravity, Radiation, and Life Support

Now, dreaming about the Moon was one thing, but turning dreams into reality? That was a whole different universe of challenges. Escape Earth's gravity? That meant mastering rocketry on a whole new level. Radiation in the vacuum of space? That posed serious health concerns. And let's not forget life support—keeping astronauts alive, healthy, and well-fed during the journey and lunar stay was no small feat.

The Lunar Seed Takes Root

As we peel back the layers of history, it's clear that the journey towards Apollo 11 didn't start with a "one giant leap." It began with daring dreams, innovative concepts, and the sheer determination to overcome every obstacle that stood in the way. From whimsical moonshot ideas to the stark reality of physics and engineering, the lunar dream began to sprout its first roots. These early sparks of imagination set the stage for the remarkable technological journey we're about to embark upon. So, get ready to explore even more chapters filled with the stories, challenges, and triumphs that made Apollo 11 the monumental success that it was!

PART II: Rocketing to the Moon

Chapter 3: The Saturn V: Engineering the Giant

Hey there, fellow space adventurers! Get ready to embark on a journey into the heart of the Apollo program's technological wonder—the awe-inspiring Saturn V rocket. Imagine a rocket so big it could make a skyscraper look like a toy! In this chapter, we're going to unveil the incredible story of how this behemoth was brought to life, from its ingenious design to its mind-boggling power.

Genesis of the Giant: Crafting a Moon-Bound Titan
The story of the Saturn V begins with NASA's vision to touch the Moon. The rocket's journey wasn't a solo mission; it was a legacy built on the shoulders of earlier rockets like the Saturn I and IB. These were like the trial runs—the prototypes that paved the way for the colossal creation that would send humans into the cosmos. The Saturn V wasn't just a machine; it was an embodiment of human ambition, a statement that we were going to reach for the stars.

Design and Layout: Building Blocks of a Lunar Odyssey

Can you picture it? A rocket soaring over 360 feet high, stretching into the sky like a skyscraper on steroids! The Saturn V was a three-stage marvel, each stage playing a vital role in the rocket's celestial ballet. The S-IC first stage, with its five monstrous F-1 engines, was all about raw power, delivering a collective thrust that could rival a small earthquake. The S-II second stage, equipped with five J-2 engines, was like the rocket's graceful dancer, elegantly guiding it towards the stars. And then came the S-IVB third stage, pushing the spacecraft out of Earth's grip and into the boundless expanse of space.

Mammoth Propulsion: The Power Within

Hold onto your helmets, because the Saturn V's engines were pure unadulterated power. The F-1 engines in the first stage? Each one spat out a staggering 1.5 million pounds of thrust! Imagine the might of five of these engines working together in perfect sync. And those J-2 engines? They used a mixture of liquid hydrogen and oxygen, a fiery concoction that unleashed a combined 1 million pounds of thrust from the second stage. The third stage's J-2 engine was like the grand finale, reigniting to shoot the spacecraft towards the Moon. It was like strapping fireworks to a skyscraper and launching it into the heavens!

During the Apollo 11 mission, the J-2 engines were primarily used in the Saturn V's S-II (second) and S-IVB (third) stages. The S-II stage was responsible for lifting the Apollo spacecraft and the S-IVB stage into Earth's orbit. Once the S-II completed its burn, it separated from the rest of the rocket, and the S-IVB stage took over.

The S-IVB stage, equipped with a single J-2 engine, performed crucial manoeuvres to send the Apollo spacecraft on its trajectory towards the Moon. It was responsible for the Trans Lunar Injection (TLI) burn, which accelerated the spacecraft out of Earth's orbit and set it on a course for the Moon.

Engineering Marvels: Overcoming Challenges

Creating the Saturn V wasn't a walk in the park—it was a puzzle of epic proportions. Engineers had to figure out how to tame the beast's weight and size, ensuring it could withstand the extreme forces of launch. They wrestled with aerodynamic forces that threatened to tear the rocket apart and vibrations that could shake it to pieces. And the F-1 engines? Those were like taming dragons; they had to withstand the fury of controlled explosions while keeping the rocket steady and safe.

The Development Process of the Apollo 11 J-2 Engines

Imagine the blueprint-filled rooms where engineers and scientists huddled, transforming vision into reality. The development of the J-2 engines involved a symphony of engineering disciplines— thermodynamics, materials science, fluid dynamics— orchestrated to craft an engine that could harness immense power while withstanding the rigours of space travel.

Turbo pumps and Thrust Chambers: Visualise the complexity of turbo pumps, elegantly designed to funnel propellants into the heart of the engine with breathtaking precision. The thrust chamber, a marvel of engineering poetry, mixed and ignited propellants to create controlled explosions that produced astonishing thrust, propelling humanity to new heights.

Testing and Iteration: Picture the controlled chaos of engine testing grounds, where prototypes underwent trial by fire. Each test was a symphony of power and control, as engineers analysed every aspect of engine performance and iterated upon their designs. Failures were met with perseverance, each setback leading to new insights and ultimately, greater success.

The Apollo 11 Ascent: Envision the culmination of

years of effort—the moment the J-2 engines roared to life beneath Saturn V's second stage, propelling Apollo 11 towards the cosmos. The controlled fury of combustion within the J-2 engines ignited a symphony of power and precision, lifting the dreams of humanity beyond Earth's bounds.

The Moon-Bound Beast Takes Flight

Picture this: July 16, 1969. The world held its breath as the Saturn V stood tall on the launchpad. The countdown echoed, and then, with a roar that could be heard for miles, the engines ignited. The rocket trembled and then lifted off, a breathtaking ballet of fire, power, and dreams. It was a moment etched into history—a moment when human determination defied gravity itself.

Legacy of a Legend: The Saturn V's Impact

The Saturn V was more than just a rocket; it was a testament to human ingenuity and audacity. Its legacy lives on, not just as a symbol of past achievements, but as a source of inspiration for the future. The rocket's groundbreaking technology pushed the boundaries of what was possible, inspiring generations of scientists, engineers, and dreamers to reach for the stars. As its engines roared and its fire blazed, the Saturn V carried not just astronauts but the hopes and aspirations of humanity, reminding us that our potential is as boundless as the cosmos itself.

Chapter 4: Countdown to Liftoff: Launch Technology

Hey there, space buffs! Buckle up, because we're about to unravel the electrifying journey from the countdown clock to the thunderous liftoff of Apollo 11. It's like the ultimate behind-the-scenes access to a Hollywood blockbuster, except this time, it's the real deal—humans soaring into the cosmos. So, grab your helmets and let's dive into the awe-inspiring world of launch technology!

Prepping for Liftoff: The Dance of Preparation
Ever tried baking a cake without following the recipe? Space travel is a bit like that, except the stakes are, well, astronomical. Months before the launch, a symphony of engineers, scientists, and technicians got to work. Every nut, bolt, and circuit had to be in perfect harmony. Think of it as assembling the most intricate puzzle ever created, with no room for missing pieces.

Simulations and Dry Runs: Rehearsing for Space
Remember the last time you practiced that dance routine for your cousin's wedding? Now imagine

doing that in space, where there's no reset button. Astronauts and mission control teams rehearsed the entire mission, sometimes running through worst-case scenarios. From launching into orbit to landing on the Moon, every step was practiced, polished, and perfected.

Countdown: The Heart-Pounding Beat of Liftoff

The countdown isn't just a catchy sequence of numbers—it's the pulse of the mission. Starting hours before launch, a complex ballet of activities unfolds. Systems are checked, fuel is loaded, and communication networks are activated. It's like getting ready for the performance of a lifetime, and each step brings us closer to that magical moment of liftoff.

Ignition Sequence: The Moment of Truth

Imagine being at a rock concert when the band finally takes the stage. Now, multiply that feeling by a million, and you might get close to the rush of liftoff. The ignition sequence is like the grand finale of the countdown—a breathtaking display of power and technology. Engines roar to life, flames erupt, and the rocket trembles under the sheer force of its engines.

Liftoff: Breaking Free of Earth's Grasp

Remember that feeling when you're on a swing, and you reach the highest point before gravity pulls you back? Now, imagine that on a cosmic scale. As the countdown hits zero, the Saturn V rocket erupts in a blaze of fire. Slowly, it defies gravity, its engines roaring louder than a thousand thunderstorms. It's a sight that leaves you breathless—a testament to human innovation and the courage to venture into the unknown.

From Countdown to Stars

The launch technology of Apollo 11 wasn't just about buttons and switches; it was about pushing the boundaries of what humanity could achieve. The countdown was a journey—a rollercoaster of tension, excitement, and anticipation. Liftoff itself was a symphony of power and dreams realised. As the Saturn V rocket pierced the skies, it carried the hopes of generations, reminding us that exploration isn't just about conquering space—it's about pushing the boundaries of what we believe is possible.

Chapter 5: Leaving Earth's Grasp: Stages of Ascent

Hey there, fellow space explorers! Prepare to embark on an exhilarating journey as we dissect the incredible stages of the Saturn V's ascent during Apollo 11. Get ready to delve deep into the heart of propulsion systems, witness the raw power of rocket engines, and experience the breathtaking voyage from our home planet to the Moon.

Liftoff: The First Step

Imagine this: The countdown reaches its dramatic conclusion, and in an eruption of fire and thunder, the Saturn V comes to life. It's like a symphony of raw power and technological prowess. The first stage, called the S-IC, roars to life with the force of five colossal F-1 engines. These beasts generate an astonishing 7.5 million pounds of thrust combined, shaking the Earth beneath them. With this explosive energy, the rocket surges off the launchpad, blazing a fiery trail into the sky.

First Stage: Conquering the Atmosphere

As the S-IC stage powers the rocket through the lower

atmosphere, its F-1 engines burn a mixture of RP-1 rocket fuel and liquid oxygen. For a little over two and a half minutes, these engines are the fiery heart of the ascent, propelling the Saturn V through the thick layers of air and into the edge of space. Once their fuel is spent, the first stage is jettisoned, shedding its weight and allowing the journey to continue.

Second Stage: Igniting the Journey

Enter the S-II stage, the second act in this cosmic drama. Now, the rocket is propelled by the grace of five J-2 engines, each guzzling a blend of liquid hydrogen and liquid oxygen. These engines may be more gentle than the F-1s, but they're no less powerful, delivering a whopping 1 million pounds of thrust each. Their combined burn lasts over six minutes, pushing the spacecraft higher and higher, inching towards the edge of our planet's gravitational grasp.

Translunar Injection: A Path to the Moon

As the second stage does its magic, the mission control team crunches the numbers for Translunar Injection (TLI). This is the moment when we say goodbye to Earth's orbit and set our sights on the Moon. The S-IVB third stage, like a cosmic conductor, reignites its single J-2 engine. This fiery burst gives the spacecraft the extra oomph it needs to escape Earth's gravitational clutches and embark on the path to lunar glory. This manoeuvre lasts just over five minutes and sets us on a trajectory that will lead us to our celestial neighbour.

Third Stage: Lunar Bound

Now, it's time for the S-IVB stage to shine. Its single J-2 engine roars back to life for about two and a half minutes, pushing the spacecraft even faster and farther away from Earth. Then, as the engine falls silent, the spacecraft enters a free coast—a quiet moment of weightlessness on the journey to the Moon. But the S-IVB stage isn't done yet; it transforms into a makeshift "space tug," guiding the Command and Service Module (CSM) towards its lunar orbit.

To Infinity and Beyond

The stages of ascent aboard the Saturn V were a symphony of power, technology, and human ingenuity. From the thunderous roar of the F-1 engines to the graceful thrust of the J-2 engines, each stage played its part in the grand drama of exploration. As we delve into the intricate details of these stages, we're reminded that the journey to the stars isn't just about defying gravity; it's about embracing our boundless curiosity, daring to venture beyond our planet's grasp, and reaching for the cosmic unknown with wide-eyed wonder.

PART III: Journey through Space

Chapter 6: Navigating the Void: Guidance and Navigation Systems

Hello, fellow cosmic adventurers! In this chapter, we're embarking on an awe-inspiring journey into the heart of the Apollo 11 mission's guidance and navigation systems. Imagine flying a spaceship through the vast expanse of space without GPS or road signs—that's the challenge the Apollo 11 team faced. Get ready to unravel the incredible technology that transformed this challenge into a triumph.

Steering by the Stars: The Necessity of Accurate Navigation

Space, the final frontier, is an unimaginably vast ocean of darkness punctuated by distant stars. Navigating through this cosmic sea required a precision that defies comparison. The guidance and navigation systems of Apollo 11 were the stellar navigators that ensured our astronauts would reach the Moon, traverse its surface, and return safely home. It wasn't just about launching a rocket; it was about charting a path through the unknown with absolute precision.

The Apollo Guidance Computer: A Brain for the Journey

Picture a room filled with blinking lights and whirring machines—the heart of Apollo 11's computing power. The onboard guidance and navigation system of the spacecraft was powered by AGC (*Apollo Guidance Computer*), a marvel of its time. With a processing speed of about 40,000 instructions per second, the AGC was revolutionary, responsible for crucial calculations and precision manoeuvres during the mission.

Fast forward to today's world where we carry more computing power in our pockets than the entire Apollo spacecraft possessed. Our smartphones boast processing speeds measured in billions of instructions per second (gigahertz), eclipsing the AGC's capabilities by orders of magnitude. Modern supercomputers are even more mind-boggling, capable of executing quadrillions (petaflops) of calculations per second.

Size and Portability: Then and Now: Imagine the AGC—a cutting-edge technological wonder of its time—occupying the space of a small refrigerator. Its portability was impressive considering the era, but it was still far from what we consider mobile today. On the other hand, modern computing devices, from smartphones to tablets, fit comfortably in the palm of our hands and offer far greater computational capabilities.

Memory: Visualise the memory capacity of the AGC, which was just 2 kilobytes of RAM (random access memory)—that's roughly equivalent to a few lines of text. In contrast, today's devices feature gigabytes or even terabytes of RAM, enabling us to store vast amounts of data, run complex applications, and multitask seamlessly.

Graphics and Interfaces: Picture the monochrome, text-based displays of the AGC. Compare that to today's vivid, high-resolution screens with capabilities ranging from 4K video playback to augmented reality experiences. The evolution in graphics and user interfaces is a testament to the strides we've made in enhancing the way we interact with technology.

The IMU, Eyes and Ears in Space: Navigating through space is like sailing blindfolded through a hurricane—there are no landmarks, and every movement matters. This is where the *Inertial Measurement Unit* (IMU) came to the rescue. Packed with gyroscopes and accelerometers, the IMU acted as the spacecraft's eyes and ears. It monitored every twist, turn, and acceleration, allowing the AGC to accurately calculate the spacecraft's position and adjust its course as needed.

The Apollo Sextant: Celestial Navigation Reimagined

Remember how ancient mariners used the stars to navigate the oceans? The Apollo Sextant brought this concept to space. Astronauts would sight on known stars using a telescope, and the AGC would work its magic to pinpoint the spacecraft's location. This celestial ballet ensured that Apollo 11 stayed on track, even in the vast cosmic expanse where Earth was just a distant glimmer.

Course Corrections: The Dance of Precision

In space, the tiniest miscalculation can lead to wildly different destinations. Imagine trying to throw a basketball into a moving net from across the street—that's the challenge of space navigation. The AGC was up to the task. It analysed the spacecraft's trajectory constantly, and if deviations occurred, it executed course corrections. It was like having a cosmic GPS that ensured the astronauts were always en route to their lunar rendezvous.

Navigating the Stars and Beyond

The guidance and navigation systems of Apollo 11 were more than just technology; they were the guardians of our astronauts' journey through the cosmos. They turned a seemingly impossible mission into a testament of human ingenuity. As we explore the depths of these systems, we're reminded that venturing into the unknown requires not just bravery, but the ability to navigate through the uncharted, guided by the same stars that have captivated our imaginations for millennia.

Chapter 7: Life in Transit: Command and Service Modules

Greetings, fellow space enthusiasts! Buckle up as we take a captivating journey inside the Apollo 11 spacecraft—the three astronauts' floating haven amidst the cosmic sea. In this chapter, we're going to dive deep into the heart of the technology that transformed their spacecraft into a temporary home, and discover the incredible living conditions that sustained them on their historic voyage to the Moon.

A Space Haven: The Command Module
Picture this: three astronauts crammed into a space not much bigger than a family car, hurtling through space at thousands of miles per hour. This was life inside the Command Module—a technological marvel engineered to endure the extreme conditions of space. It wasn't just a vessel; it was their lifeline, their fortress against the cosmic void. Within its walls, they communicated, navigated, and found a slice of normalcy amidst the stars.

Apollo 11 Astronauts: Neil Armstrong, Buzz Aldrin, and Michael Collins

Get ready to journey through the cosmos of history as we delve into the lives and contributions of the incredible trio who made the Apollo 11 mission an enduring symbol of human achievement: Neil Armstrong, Buzz Aldrin, and Michael Collins. These names are synonymous with courage, discovery, and the unyielding human spirit that pushed the boundaries of exploration to new celestial heights.

Neil Armstrong - The Emblematic Pioneer: Neil Armstrong, the intrepid commander of Apollo 11, etched his name into history as the first person to set foot on the Moon's surface. With his steady nerves and laser-focused determination, Armstrong's "That's one small step for [a] man, one giant leap for mankind" will forever echo through the corridors of time. A pilot and engineer, Armstrong epitomised the quiet, unassuming hero who stood on the shoulders of countless visionaries to reach for the stars.

Buzz Aldrin - The Luminary Lunar Explorer: Enter Buzz Aldrin, the lunar module pilot who followed Armstrong onto the Moon. With a deep passion for space exploration, Aldrin's enthusiasm for the cosmos was palpable. He conducted scientific experiments, collected lunar samples, and left his own footprint on history. A remarkable engineer and astronaut, Aldrin's journey to the Moon was a testament to humanity's relentless pursuit of knowledge and adventure beyond Earth's boundaries.

Michael Collins - The Cosmic Connector: Amid the lunar excitement, there was Michael Collins, the command module pilot—an astronaut whose name might not be as widely known but whose role was equally essential. Collins circled the Moon in solitude, maintaining vital communication between the lunar surface and mission control. His reflection on the far side of the Moon, hidden from both Earth and his companions, offered a glimpse into the solitude and introspection that define space travel.

The legacy of these three astronauts—Armstrong, Aldrin, and Collins—is not just a story of space exploration; it's a tapestry woven from the threads of human spirit, daring, and collaboration. Their names inspire us to embrace the unknown, to step beyond our comfort zones, and to reach for the stars. As we celebrate their remarkable journey, we're reminded that the cosmic voyage isn't just about technology and discovery; it's about the human story—a story of aspiration, unity, and the ever-burning desire to explore the cosmos and unravel its mysteries.

Life Support Systems: Breathing Easy in the Cosmos

Breathing in space is a tad more complicated than on Earth. That's where the *Environmental Control System* (ECS) stepped in. This intricate marvel managed the spacecraft's internal environment, ensuring the temperature was just right, humidity levels were optimal, and oxygen was replenished. It's like having your very own atmospheric butler, making sure you can breathe easy and stay comfortable in the vacuum of space.

Navigating the Stars: Guidance and Control

Imagine piloting a spacecraft to the Moon using manual controls—talk about a cosmic challenge! The Apollo Guidance and Navigation System acted as the astronauts' guiding star. It was their cosmic compass, ensuring they stayed on course and making precision adjustments to their trajectory. Think of it as the ultimate GPS, steering them through the celestial seas with unerring accuracy.

Cosmic Cuisine: Dining Among the Stars

Now, let's talk food. Gourmet meals weren't on the menu, but the culinary ingenuity was still impressive. Food was vacuum-sealed into convenient packages, including freeze-dried delights like scrambled eggs and chicken stew. These space bites were rehydrated with precious water—a commodity as valuable as gold in space. Imagine sipping on a pouch of water to turn powdery eggs into a cosmic feast.

Rest and Relaxation: Sleeping in Zero-G

Sleeping in zero gravity? It might sound like a dream, but it has its quirks. Astronauts didn't have beds; they had sleeping bags that could attach to the walls. Imagine snoozing while floating—a kind of cosmic lullaby. Sleeping in space meant there was no "up" or "down," allowing the astronauts to slumber in whatever position felt most comfortable.

Keeping Connected: Communication with Earth

As the Apollo 11 spacecraft ventured to lunar distances, staying connected with mission control was paramount. Sophisticated communication systems enabled the astronauts to stay in touch with Earth, sharing updates, receiving instructions, and ensuring a lifeline to home. It was like having a direct line to Earth's heart, no matter how far they traveled.

A Home Beyond the Sky

The Apollo 11 spacecraft wasn't just a vessel; it was a sanctuary of technology that sustained its occupants through a groundbreaking journey. It was a microcosm of human ingenuity, showcasing our ability to create a temporary haven in the boundless void. As we uncover the details of their living conditions, we're reminded that space exploration isn't just about reaching new frontiers—it's about adapting to the unknown, making a home among the stars, and revealing the incredible potential of human innovation in the face of challenges that span the cosmos.

Chapter 8: Communication Across the Cosmos

Hey there, fellow space enthusiasts! Buckle up as we embark on a fascinating journey into the world of communication systems that linked Apollo 11 with our beautiful blue planet. Get ready to explore the technological marvels that allowed astronauts to stay connected, share their awe-inspiring experiences, and maintain an unbreakable lifeline across the vast cosmic expanse.

A Cosmic Connection: The Importance of Communication

Imagine floating in the cold vacuum of space, millions of miles away from home. What would you long for the most? Communication, the lifeline to humanity. The communication systems of Apollo 11 were like a cosmic telephone line that spanned the chasm between the spacecraft and mission control. They weren't just tools; they were the heartbeat of the mission, enabling vital exchanges of information that ensured the success and safety of the astronauts.

The Tracking Network: Ears to the Skies

To send messages across the cosmos, NASA set up the *Deep Space Network* (DSN), a global network of massive radio antennas. These colossal dishes, stationed in California, Spain, and Australia, were the cosmic ears that listened to the spacecraft's signals. They tracked the spacecraft's position, received data, and sent commands—a symphony of technology that operated at the speed of light, connecting two worlds separated by the vast expanse of space.

Voice and Data: Talking and Texting with the Stars

Communication wasn't just about ones and zeros; it was about sharing voices and experiences. The Apollo 11 crew used the Unified S-Band communication system to send their voices and critical data back to Earth. Neil Armstrong's iconic words, Buzz Aldrin's descriptions of the lunar surface, and the constant stream of data about the spacecraft's health traveled through the vacuum of space, bringing the astronauts' presence to people around the world.

The Lunar Module's Link: The Lunar Module Adapter

As Apollo 11 descended to the Moon's surface, an essential link was established through the Lunar Module Adapter (LMA). This technological bridge connected the Command Module with the Lunar Module, ensuring seamless data exchange and instructions between the two spacecraft. It was a pivotal connection that enabled the LM to descend to the lunar surface and return safely to rendezvous with the orbiting Command Module.

The S-band communication system was a vital technology used for data exchange between the Command Module (CM) and the Lunar Module (LM) during the Apollo missions, including Apollo 11. This system operated in the S-band radio frequency range, and it played a crucial role in transmitting voice, telemetry data, and other mission-critical information between the two spacecraft. Here's a description of the S-band link technology:

1. S-Band Frequency Range: The S-band communication system operates in a frequency range between 2 and 4 gigahertz (GHz). This frequency range was chosen because it strikes a balance between the ability to transmit data over relatively long distances and the ability to penetrate Earth's atmosphere and lunar vacuum effectively.

2. S-Band Antennas: Both the CM and LM were equipped with S-band antennas for transmitting and receiving data. These antennas were designed to be highly directional, allowing for precise targeting of signals between the two spacecraft and with Earth-based tracking stations.

3. Voice Communication: The S-band system facilitated voice communication between the astronauts in the CM and LM. This allowed them to communicate with each other and with mission control on Earth. Voice data was transmitted as analog signals over the S-band frequencies.

4. Telemetry Data: Telemetry data, which included information about the health and status of various spacecraft systems, was also transmitted over the S-band link. This data was crucial for monitoring the spacecraft's performance and making real-time adjustments during the mission.

5. Data Modulation: To transmit voice and telemetry data efficiently, the S-band system used various modulation techniques. Amplitude Modulation (AM) was commonly used for voice communication, while Frequency Modulation (FM) and Phase Modulation (PM) were employed for telemetry data.

6. Tracking and Ranging: The S-band link was essential for tracking and ranging purposes. Earth-based tracking stations used the S-band signals to precisely determine the spacecraft's position and velocity. This data was crucial for navigation and ensuring that the spacecraft followed the planned trajectory.

7. Omnidirectional and High-Gain Antennas: The S-band system on both the CM and LM included omnidirectional antennas for communication when the two spacecraft were in close proximity, such as during docking and undocking maneuvers. High-gain antennas were used for long-distance communication, ensuring a strong and reliable signal over greater distances.

8. Signal Strength and Power: The S-band system employed high-power transmitters to ensure that signals could travel across the vast distances between the Moon and Earth. The strength of the S-band signal was critical for maintaining a robust connection.

9. Redundancy: Redundancy was built into the S-band communication system to ensure reliability. In the event of a system failure, the spacecraft could switch to backup equipment to maintain communication with mission control.

The S-band link was a lifeline for the astronauts and mission control, allowing for real-time communication and data exchange between the CM, LM, and Earth-based support teams. This technology represented a remarkable achievement in the field of space communication and played a crucial role in the success of the Apollo program, including the historic Apollo 11 mission.

Lifeline to Earth: Voice and Video

The communication systems didn't just transmit data; they shared emotions, experiences, and historic moments. With the flip of a switch, astronauts could send their voices, images, and even video footage back to Earth. As Neil Armstrong took that "one small step," his words resonated across the cosmos, and the world shared in the moment of human triumph. It was more than communication; it was a bridge that united us all.

Part IV: Approaching the Moon

Chapter 9: Docking and Lunar Module Extraction

Hey there, fellow space adventurers! Hold onto your helmets as we take a deep dive into the exciting world of docking and lunar module extraction—essential phases that made Apollo 11's historic lunar landing possible. Get ready to unveil the mesmerising choreography and remarkable technology that enabled two spacecraft to link up in the cosmic dance of exploration.

A Cosmic Connection: Docking the Command and Lunar Modules

Imagine two spacecraft suspended in space, about to perform an extraordinary cosmic ballet. Docking was the moment these space voyagers connected in the black void. The Command Module reached out with its docking probe, while the Lunar Module extended its drogue—an intricate handshake that joined these metal giants. The docking probe nestled into the drogue, forming a secure and vital link between the modules.

The Docking Probe and Drogue: Handshake in Space

Docking wasn't just about locking parts together; it was about creating a bridge for the astronauts to move between the modules. The Command Module's docking probe extended like a mechanical arm, while the Lunar Module's drogue acted as a guide. As they touched, the two spacecraft became one—a connection in the infinite abyss. Think of it like locking hands with a friend across a cosmic divide.

Pressure Equalisation: Bridging the Gap

Before astronauts could move between the modules, the pressure had to be balanced. The hatch connecting the Command and Lunar Modules was about to swing open—but space is a vacuum, and sudden pressure changes could be catastrophic. A delicate dance of valves and controls ensured that pressure equalised gradually, preventing a sudden rush of air from turning into a cosmic whirlwind.

Lunar Module Extraction: Releasing the Lunar Module

Picture this: the Moon beckoning in the distance, and it's time to release the Lunar Module—a trusty companion that would soon touch the lunar surface. Extracting the Lunar Module was a carefully timed manoeuvre. It had to be gently detached from the Command Module, allowing it to start its solo journey around the Moon. It was like sending a child off to explore a distant playground.

Burn and Release: Setting the Stage for Lunar Descent

As the Lunar Module settled into its lunar orbit, it was time for a key manoeuvre. The Lunar Module's engine roared to life, executing a Trans-Earth Injection (TEI) burn. This burn boosted its speed, sending it on a trajectory back towards Earth. With the burn complete, the Lunar Module was released from the Command Module—a moment of separation that marked the next step on its incredible journey.

Docking the Command and Lunar Modules: A Delicate Cosmic Ballet

The docking process of the Command Module (CM) and Lunar Module (LM) during the Apollo missions, including Apollo 11, was a meticulously choreographed sequence of steps. This delicate cosmic ballet required precision and coordination to ensure a secure connection between the two spacecraft. Here's a detailed description of the process and steps involved:

Step 1 - Undocking Preparation (Post-Lunar Orbit): Before the docking procedure begins, the two spacecraft, CM and LM, are already in lunar orbit. The LM has just completed its descent to the lunar surface and is ready to ascend back to the CM. The steps leading up to the docking process are as follows:

-LM Ascent Stage Activation: The ascent stage of the LM is activated, and its systems are checked to ensure it's ready for rendezvous and docking.

-LM's Ascent Burn: A precisely calculated ascent burn is initiated on the LM's ascent stage to lift off from the lunar surface. This burn aligns the LM's trajectory with that of the CM in lunar orbit.

-CM's Orbit Keeping: Meanwhile, the CM remains in lunar orbit, performing orbital manoeuvres to maintain its position and prepare for rendezvous with the ascending LM.

Step 2 - Rendezvous and Approach: Once the ascent stage of the LM has lifted off from the lunar surface, the process of rendezvous with the CM begins. This involves a carefully planned sequence of steps to bring the two spacecraft together:

-Initial Phasing Burn: The LM's ascent stage performs

an initial burn to adjust its trajectory and align its orbit with that of the CM.

-Midcourse Corrections: If necessary, midcourse correction burns may be performed by both the LM and CM to fine-tune their trajectories and ensure a precise rendezvous.

-Terminal Phase Initiation: As the LM approaches the CM, it enters the terminal phase of rendezvous. This phase involves the LM's onboard guidance and navigation systems aligning it with the CM.

-Radar Tracking: Both spacecraft use radar systems to track each other's position and relative velocity accurately. This data is essential for making real-time adjustments to the approach.

Step 3: Docking Manoeuvre: As the LM gets closer to the CM, the actual docking manoeuvre takes place. This is a carefully orchestrated process with multiple steps:

-Initial Capture: The LM's probe and drogue system extends towards the CM's docking collar. The probe is designed to fit into the drogue, providing an initial capture and alignment between the two spacecraft.

-Soft Docking: Once the probe and drogue are engaged, the LM's thrusters are used to gently bring the two spacecraft closer together. The docking latches on the CM and LM gradually engage, creating a secure connection.

-Hard Docking: After the soft docking is complete, the final hard docking is achieved when pyrotechnic devices on both spacecraft fire, creating a secure, airtight seal between the CM and LM.

Step 4 - Post-Docking Procedures: With the CM and LM successfully docked, the astronauts can transfer between the two spacecraft. This transition allows the lunar module crew, who have spent time on the moon's surface, to rejoin the command module pilot in the CM for the journey back to Earth.

-Hatch Opening: The astronauts open the hatches separating the CM and LM, allowing them to move freely between the two spacecraft.

-Transfer of Astronauts and Samples: The astronauts transfer from the LM to the CM, bringing with them lunar samples and data collected during their time on the moon.

Step 5 - Lunar Module Descent Stage Separation: Once the transfer of astronauts and samples is complete, the LM's descent stage, which is no longer needed, is separated and left in lunar orbit. Only the ascent stage of the LM remains attached to the CM for the journey back to Earth.

Docking the Command and Lunar Modules was a critical and complex procedure during the Apollo missions, requiring meticulous planning, precise navigation, and skilled execution by the astronauts and mission control. It was a pivotal moment that marked the transition from lunar surface operations to the journey home, ensuring the safe return of the astronauts to Earth.

Chapter 10: Precision Manoeuvres: Apollo 11 Course Corrections and Lunar Orbit Insertion

Hey there, cosmic adventurers! Buckle up for a thrilling journey into the mesmerising world of precision manoeuvres that guided Apollo 11 to its rendezvous with the Moon. In this chapter, we're going to explore the mind-boggling technology and exhilarating calculations that allowed astronauts to tweak their course and gracefully slide into lunar orbit.

Setting the Stage: Course Corrections on the Cosmic Highway

Imagine piloting a spacecraft through the vast expanse of space—a journey that's like threading a needle from millions of miles away. Course corrections were the cosmic steering wheel, the tools that fine-tuned Apollo 11's trajectory toward the lunar bullseye. With the Moon as their guidepost, astronauts relied on calculated engine burns to ensure they stayed on the cosmic highway, inching closer to their lunar destination.

The Stellar Navigation System: Guiding by the Stars

This wasn't guesswork; it was a symphony of calculations and celestial navigation. The star-studded canvas of space wasn't just beautiful; it was functional. The Apollo Guidance Computer (AGC) acted as a cosmic GPS, using star sightings and data from the Inertial Measurement Unit (IMU) to triangulate the spacecraft's precise position. It's like finding your way on Earth using landmarks, but with a sprinkle of celestial magic.

Mid-Course Corrections: Nudging Toward the Moon

Even the tiniest deviations could snowball into cosmic detours. So, mid-course corrections were like cosmic nudges to keep Apollo 11 on track. These precise engine burns were like whispers from mission control —calculated, timed, and executed with perfection. Think of it as tapping the steering wheel ever so slightly to keep your car in the right lane, except this was done from millions of miles away.

Lunar Orbit Insertion: Slipping into the Moon's Gravitational Embrace

Entering lunar orbit was a breathtaking ballet between spacecraft and celestial body. The Moon's gravitational embrace could capture the spacecraft, but only if the timing and speed were spot on. The Lunar Orbit

Insertion (LOI) burn was the crescendo. With hearts racing and calculations humming, the engine roared to life, gently slowing the spacecraft to be captured by the Moon's gravity, gracefully slipping into lunar orbit.

From Earth to Lunar Orbit Insertion - A Cosmic Odyssey

Imagine a hot July morning in 1969 at the Kennedy Space Center in Florida. The anticipation was palpable as the world watched the culmination of years of planning and hard work—the launch of Apollo 11, humanity's bold attempt to reach the Moon. Here, we embark on a detailed journey from Earth to the monumental Lunar Orbit Insertion (LOI) during the Apollo 11 mission, a story of innovation, precision, and human determination.

Day 1: Launch and Earth Orbit - On July 16, 1969, at 09:32 EDT, the Saturn V rocket, towering at 363 feet, thundered to life, defying Earth's gravity. This iconic launch marked the beginning of Apollo 11's epic voyage. The spacecraft swiftly reached low Earth orbit, where astronauts Neil Armstrong, Buzz Aldrin, and Michael Collins felt the first sensations of weightlessness and witnessed the curvature of our planet.

Day 2: Translunar Injection (TLI) and Coast to the Moon - The following day, July 16, at 16:22 EDT, Apollo 11 executed the Translunar Injection burn. The third-stage engine roared to life once more, propelling the spacecraft beyond Earth's grasp and setting it on course for the Moon. The crew found themselves in the vast emptiness of space, coasting toward their lunar destination.

Days 3-4: Coast to the Moon - During this period of coasting through space, the astronauts conducted a delicate cosmic ballet of system checks and navigational adjustments. They also devoted time to scientific experiments, contributing to our understanding of the space environment.

Day 4: Lunar Module (LM) Activation and Systems Check - July 19 was a pivotal day as preparations for lunar descent began. The Lunar Module, affectionately named "Eagle," was extracted from the Saturn V's third stage. With great care, the LM's systems were activated and checked meticulously to ensure it was ready for its momentous descent to the lunar surface.

Day 5: Lunar Orbit Insertion (LOI) Burn - July 19, 17:21 EDT—a moment that held the world's breath. The Lunar Orbit Insertion burn commenced, a six-minute-long engine burn that slowed Apollo 11 down enough to be captured by the Moon's gravity. It was a critical manoeuvre that had to be executed with precision to ensure the spacecraft entered lunar orbit successfully. The world watched in awe as this breathtaking manoeuvre marked Apollo 11's arrival in lunar orbit.

Days 5-6: Lunar Orbit and Preparations for Descent - Apollo 11 settled into a stable lunar orbit, a cosmic dance with the Moon. The astronauts, now in lunar orbit, conducted final checks and made preparations for the momentous descent to the lunar surface. Instruments were calibrated, checklists reviewed, and nerves of steel honed.

The Dance of Mathematics and Motion

Precision manoeuvres were more than just engine burns; they were a masterpiece of mathematics and motion. The technology that allowed Apollo 11 to adjust its course and embrace lunar orbit was a testament to human ingenuity and the harmony between science and engineering. As we uncover the details of these manoeuvres, we're reminded that space exploration is a symphony of calculated steps, a dance of innovation that allows us to pirouette among the stars and leave our mark on the cosmic stage.

Part V: Descent and Landing

Chapter 11: The Eagle Has Landed: Lunar Module Descent

Hey there, cosmic adventurers! Get ready for a pulse-pounding journey as we dive into the thrilling climax of Apollo 11's mission—the mesmerising lunar module descent. In this chapter, we're going to unveil the heart-stopping sequence of events that brought Neil Armstrong and Buzz Aldrin to the Moon's surface, exposing the incredible technology, meticulous planning, and sheer courage that defined humanity's audacious first steps on an alien world.

A Lunar Ballet: Setting the Stage for Descent
Picture this: the Moon's surface slowly creeping into view beneath you—a landscape untouched by human feet. As the Lunar Module, nicknamed "Eagle," separated from the Command Module, it was like breaking away from the cosmic waltz of space. Inside, Armstrong and Aldrin were about to embark on a gravity-defying ballet, where engines and calculations would determine their destiny.

Powered Descent Initiation: The Heart of the Descent

The descent kicked off with the Powered Descent Initiation (PDI) burn—a heart-pounding moment where the Lunar Module's descent engine fired, slowing its descent. It wasn't just about shedding speed; it was about achieving a delicate balance between control and daring. Armstrong and Aldrin, hands on the controls, had the lunar landscape in their sights as they guided the Lunar Module toward a historic landing.

Vertical Descent and Hover: Precision Meets Skill

Descending toward the Moon's surface was a blend of technological marvels and human skill. Radar systems and onboard computers worked in tandem, constantly calculating altitude and descent rates. The on-board computer, the "AGC," was a marvel of its time, executing complex algorithms to guide the descent. Armstrong's precise piloting and the AGC's calculations turned the Lunar Module into a hovering masterpiece, as they aimed for the perfect landing spot.

The 1202 Alarm: A Heart-Stopping Moment

Imagine the tension in the cockpit as an unfamiliar alarm—1202—sounded. It was a moment of uncertainty, but Armstrong's training and the guidance of mission control shone through. The AGC's multitasking prowess kicked in, allowing Armstrong to continue the descent. The 1202 alarm, caused by data overload, was like a hiccup in an otherwise flawless sequence. With calm determination, the descent continued toward the lunar surface.

The Eagle Has Landed: Touchdown on Another World

Finally, with bated breath, as the Lunar Module's shadow kissed the lunar soil, history was made. With less than half a minute of fuel left, Armstrong deftly guided the Lunar Module to a safe landing site. The "Eagle" gently settled onto the Moon's surface. Armstrong's iconic words—"Houston, Tranquility Base here. The Eagle has landed"—echoed across space. The lunar module's landing legs absorbed the impact, and the dream of touching the Moon became a triumphant reality.

A Cosmic Ballet of Valour and Ingenuity

The lunar module descent was more than a technical ballet; it was a symphony of courage and innovation. The technology that allowed Armstrong and Aldrin to navigate the alien atmosphere and land safely was a testament to human genius. As we unravel the details of this descent, we're reminded that space exploration isn't just about reaching new horizons; it's about pushing boundaries, defying gravity, and etching our legacy onto the Moon's surface and the annals of human achievement.

Chapter 12: Touchdown on Tranquility: Lunar Landing Technology

Hey there, cosmic explorers! Brace yourselves for a mind-blowing journey into the heart of lunar landing technology—the magical realm where innovation and courage merged to turn Apollo 11's audacious dream of touching the Moon into an awe-inspiring reality. Join us as we peel back the layers of technology that allowed Neil Armstrong and Buzz Aldrin to make their historic touchdown on the lunar soil.

A Lunar Odyssey: Approaching Tranquility Base
Imagine looking out of the Lunar Module's window as the Moon's rugged landscape gradually consumes your view—a breathtaking panorama of craters and mysteries. The world watched with bated breath as "Eagle" descended towards Tranquility Base, a site chosen for its safety and scientific value. But this descent wasn't just about landing; it was about making history, and technology was the magic wand.

Landing Radar: Gazing at the Moon's Surface
As the Lunar Module delicately descended, a

technological marvel came into play—the Lunar Module Descent and Landing Radar (LM-DL). This radar system emitted waves that danced off the lunar terrain and returned as valuable echoes. By analysing the time it took for these signals to bounce back, the onboard computer calculated altitude and speed, steering the Lunar Module towards a precise landing site.

Programmed Descent: The AGC's Stellar Performance

Visualise the Lunar Module gracefully descending towards the Moon's surface—a ballet of science and engineering. The true maestro here was the Apollo Guidance Computer (AGC). Loaded with landing algorithms, the AGC ensured that the descent trajectory was smooth and controlled. It wasn't just ones and zeros; it was a symphony of calculations that translated into Neil Armstrong and Buzz Aldrin inching closer to their historic landing.

P66 and P64: The Dance of Descent

As the Lunar Module continued its descent, two pivotal moments—P66 and P64—stood between it and the lunar surface. P66 was the magical shift from vertical to horizontal guidance, aligning the Lunar Module's attitude perfectly for the final descent. P64, the final approach phase, ensured that the spacecraft was gliding gracefully to its chosen landing spot. Think of it as a pilot's graceful swoop before a picture-perfect touchdown.

The 30-Second Countdown: Fuel and Fate

In the final moments of descent, imagine Neil Armstrong and Buzz Aldrin having just 30 seconds of fuel left. The clock was ticking, and every second counted. With precision that defied belief, they skilfully managed their descent, navigating towards the landing site while their hearts raced. And then it happened—the Lunar Module's landing legs kissed the lunar surface, etching humanity's mark on the Moon.

The Eagle's Descent to the Moon: A Thrilling Lunar Ballet

The descent of the Lunar Module (LM) "Eagle" to the Moon during the Apollo 11 mission was a high-stakes, meticulously planned ballet of engineering precision and astronaut skill. Here's a detailed description of the steps and timing involved in this historic journey:

Step 1: Initiation of Descent (Day 5)

Mission Day 5: The day begins in lunar orbit. The LM, with astronauts Neil Armstrong and Buzz Aldrin onboard, is nestled in the lunar module's descent stage, while Michael Collins orbits above in the Command Module.

Initiating Descent: Armstrong and Aldrin, having completed their checks and preparations, initiate the descent sequence. They're poised for the descent to the lunar surface.

Step 2: Powered Descent Initiation (PDI)

PDI Burn (Day 5): As the LM approaches the lunar surface, the descent engine is fired up for the Powered Descent Initiation (PDI) burn. This critical maneuver precisely adjusts the LM's trajectory to guide it toward the chosen landing site within the Sea of Tranquility.

Step 3: Powered Descent and Descent Phase

Powered Descent: The LM enters a powered descent phase, gradually decreasing its altitude and velocity. Armstrong and Aldrin carefully monitor their instruments, making real-time adjustments to ensure a safe descent.

Descent Stage Jettison: After the LM's descent engine has done its job, the descent stage, which provided the necessary thrust, is jettisoned. The LM's ascent stage, with its iconic spidery legs, is now the sole occupant of the lunar journey.

Step 4: Pitch Over and Hover

Pitch Over: As the LM gets closer to the surface, it performs a pitch-over manoeuvre to position itself horizontally and prepare for a controlled horizontal translation.

Hovering: The LM reaches a critical point called "hover" when it's just a few hundred feet above the lunar surface. At this point, Armstrong takes manual control of the spacecraft.

Step 5: Selection of Landing Site
Site Selection: Armstrong realises that the original landing site is strewn with large boulders. With limited fuel and mere seconds before touchdown, he makes a quick decision to override the automatic guidance system and manually fly the LM to a safer landing site.

Step 6: Touchdown (Day 6)
Final Descent: Armstrong expertly pilots the LM to the new landing site. The LM's shadow races across the lunar surface as the moment of touchdown nears.

Touchdown (July 20, 1969, 20:17 EDT): With less than 30 seconds of fuel remaining, the LM gently touches down on the lunar surface. Neil Armstrong famously utters, "The Eagle has landed." The world watches in awe as humanity takes its first step onto another celestial body.

Step 7: Shutdown and Preparations for Lunar Walk

Engine Shutdown: With the LM safely on the Moon, the descent engine is shut down. The LM's systems are prepared for the lunar walk, and the astronauts begin donning their space suits and preparing for their historic moonwalk.

The descent of the Lunar Module "Eagle" to the Moon was a heart-pounding adventure of engineering prowess, cool-headed astronaut decision-making, and historic significance. It marked the culmination of years of planning and effort, making Neil Armstrong and Buzz Aldrin the first humans to set foot on another world, forever changing our perspective of the cosmos.

Crafting History with Cutting-Edge Artistry

Apollo 11's lunar landing wasn't just a feat of engineering; it was a testament to the brilliance of human creativity and innovation. The Landing Radar, AGC, and the intricate algorithms were the unsung heroes of this momentous event. As we delve into the depths of this lunar landing technology, we're reminded that space exploration isn't just about reaching destinations; it's about turning dreams into reality, using technology to sculpt history, and proving that even the most audacious visions can be transformed into tangible, awe-inspiring achievements in the boundless canvas of the cosmos.

Part VI: Walking on the Moon

Chapter 13: First Steps: The Space Suit and Extravehicular Mobility Unit

Greetings, fellow space enthusiasts! Buckle up for an exhilarating journey into the world of space fashion—where high-tech suits became the heroes that allowed humans to take their historic first steps on the Moon. In this chapter, we're diving deep into the awe-inspiring technology behind the space suits and Extravehicular Mobility Units (EMUs) that turned ordinary astronauts into lunar pioneers.

A Cosmic Wardrobe: Designing for the Void

Imagine standing on the lunar surface, surrounded by the barren beauty of the Moon, but also facing its hostile environment—vacuum, extreme temperatures, and a distinct lack of breathable air. This wasn't a fashion show; this was about survival. The space suit was more than just a uniform; it was a mini spaceship, a life-support system that would keep astronauts safe, comfortable, and functional in the cosmic wilderness.

Lunar Environment: Extreme and Unchanging

Imagine stepping out of the Lunar Module Eagle onto the surface of the Moon. It's an otherworldly experience, and the lunar environment is unlike anything you've ever encountered on Earth. Here's a friendly, detailed exploration:

Temperature Extremes: The Moon's surface experiences jaw-dropping temperature extremes. During the lunar day, which lasts for about two Earth weeks, the thermometer can rocket up to a scorching 127 degrees Celsius (260 degrees Fahrenheit). It's like being in an oven!

Then, when the lunar night sets in for another two-week period, temperatures plummet dramatically. The Moon's lack of an atmosphere means there's no blanket to trap heat, so nighttime temperatures can plunge to a bone-chilling -173 degrees Celsius (-280 degrees Fahrenheit). It's colder than the coldest winter night in Antarctica.

No Atmosphere, No Weather: Unlike Earth, where we have a dynamic atmosphere with weather systems, clouds, and wind, the Moon is devoid of such features. It has practically no atmosphere to speak of. That means no rain, no storms, and definitely no wind to rustle your hair.

Harsh Sunlight: The bright side of the Moon, when the Sun is up, can be blindingly bright. The Moon's surface reflects sunlight brilliantly, and without an atmosphere to scatter or filter it, the sunlight is unforgivingly intense.

No Liquid Water: Due to the extreme temperatures and the lack of an atmosphere to maintain pressure, liquid water cannot exist on the Moon's surface. Any water that might be present is locked in the form of ice in permanently shadowed craters at the Moon's poles.

Soundless Silence: Because there's no atmosphere to transmit sound waves, the lunar surface is eerily silent. No one can hear you speak or any sounds you might make, even if you could survive without a spacesuit (which, of course, you can't).

No Protection from Space Hazards: One of the more challenging aspects of the lunar environment is its lack of protection from space hazards. With no atmosphere to shield against solar radiation or micrometeoroids, the lunar surface is constantly bombarded by these potentially harmful elements.

So, when the Lunar Module Eagle touched down on the Moon during the Apollo 11 mission, it was in a realm of extremes and stillness. The astronauts had to rely on their specially designed spacesuits, equipment, and extensive training to navigate and conduct their historic moonwalk. It was an adventure into the unknown, and their footsteps marked humanity's first foray into the lunar wilderness, forever changing our understanding of what's possible in space exploration.

Layers of Protection: Crafting the Ultimate Armour

Let's peel back the layers—literally—of the space suit. Imagine astronauts suiting up, layer by layer, each with a specific purpose. The innermost layer provided thermal insulation to maintain body temperature. The middle layers shielded against micrometeoroids and radiation, acting as cosmic bodyguards. The outer layer was a multi-material masterpiece, a composite armour shielding against the unforgiving vacuum.

The Helmet: A Gateway to Discovery

Visualise astronauts gazing out through their helmet visors—like windows to another world. The helmet wasn't just a portal; it was a guardian. It protected their eyes from the blinding sunlight, shielded them from tiny space debris, and gave them an unobstructed view of their lunar surroundings. The visor's gold coating even reflected sunlight, preventing overheating while letting astronauts drink in the cosmic vista.

Life Support Backpack: Heartbeat of Exploration

Picture the backpack—known as the Portable Life

Support System (PLSS)—strapped to the astronaut's back. It wasn't just a load; it was life itself. It carried the essential components: oxygen supply, carbon dioxide scrubbers, cooling systems, and communication gear. This backpack ensured astronauts could breathe, stay cool, communicate with mission control, and make history on the lunar terrain.

Extravehicular Mobility Unit (EMU): A Symphony of Engineering

The Extravehicular Mobility Unit (EMU) was like a tailor-made spacecraft for lunar exploration. Imagine astronauts clad in these advanced exoskeletons, each designed for maximum mobility. With articulated joints, life support systems, communication gear, and a visor connecting them to the lunar panorama, the EMU turned ordinary humans into cosmic explorers with agility and grace.

Mobility on the Moon: Dance of Discovery

Imagine the sensation of walking on the Moon—the suit's joints moving, the lunar dust floating in the airless environment. The EMU's flexible design allowed astronauts to perform delicate tasks like collecting samples and setting up experiments. It wasn't just a suit; it was an extension of the human body, a conduit that translated the explorer's intention into cosmic action.

Enabling the Extraordinary

The space suit and Extravehicular Mobility Unit weren't just protective gear; they were the keys to unlocking humanity's dreams of exploring the Moon. The painstaking design, the layers of technology, and the ingenious engineering transformed these suits into the guardians of history. As we delve into these spacefaring garments, we're reminded that space exploration isn't just about equipment—it's about the audacity to explore, the human spirit that refuses to be bound, and the tangible proof that innovation knows no limits, even in the boundless expanse of space.

Part VII: Scientific Exploration

Chapter 14: Lunar Science Tools: Equipment and Instruments

Hello, fellow space aficionados! Prepare to be utterly captivated as we embark on a journey through the remarkable arsenal of scientific tools that propelled Apollo 11's lunar adventure into the realm of scientific wonders. In this chapter, we're about to uncover the ingenious instruments that transformed Neil Armstrong and Buzz Aldrin into cosmic investigators, unraveling the mysteries of the Moon like never before.

Astronomer's Delight: Instruments of Lunar Exploration

Imagine stepping onto the Moon's surface, equipped with a treasure trove of instruments that would make any scientist's heart race with excitement. But these were no ordinary tools; they were the culmination of human ingenuity—scientific marvels designed to unlock the secrets of the lunar realm.

The Apollo Lunar Surface Experiments Package (ALSEP): Our Lunar Laboratory

At the heart of Apollo 11's scientific arsenal stood the

Apollo Lunar Surface Experiments Package (ALSEP) —a symphony of instruments poised to transform the Moon's surface into a laboratory of cosmic insights. This package was the astronaut's legacy; it remained on the Moon after their departure, tirelessly collecting data to this day. ALSEP's sensors measured seismic activity, temperature variations, and cosmic rays, shedding light on the Moon's geophysical properties and its interactions with the universe.

Solar Wind Composition Experiment: Capturing Sunlight's Whispers

Imagine capturing particles from the Sun—the very essence of its existence. The Solar Wind Composition Experiment allowed astronauts to do just that. By exposing collector panels to the solar wind, scientists gained insights into the Sun's elemental composition and the nature of its energy stream. This experiment provided a direct link between our planet and our parent star, helping us understand the Sun's role in shaping the Moon's surface.

Lunar Seismic Profiling: Echoes of Moonquakes

Picture this: seismic sensors embedded in lunar soil, waiting for the Moon to send forth rumbles of its geological history. These sensors formed the Lunar Seismic Profiling experiment. By studying the seismic waves generated by Moonquakes, scientists gained a peek into the Moon's interior structure, learning about its composition, crustal thickness, and even its core.

Soil Mechanics Surface Sampler: Lunar Soil Up Close

Imagine scooping up lunar soil, not just for its lunar beauty, but for scientific exploration. The Soil Mechanics Surface Sampler allowed astronauts to do exactly that. This tool collected soil samples from various depths, unveiling insights into the Moon's geological history, its regolith's behaviour, and the processes that shaped its surface over eons.

Laser Ranging Retroreflector: The Moon's Own Beacon

Consider placing a retroreflector on the Moon—a device that bounces back light exactly from where it came. The Laser Ranging Retroreflector was precisely that. This small device, placed on the lunar surface, enabled scientists on Earth to send laser beams to the Moon and measure the time it took for the light to return. This experiment wasn't just about measuring distance; it gave us an unprecedented understanding of the Moon's orbit, its relationship with Earth, and even the nature of gravity itself.

Instruments of Cosmic Revelation

The instruments and tools that accompanied Apollo 11's astronauts were more than just mechanisms; they were instruments of cosmic revelation. From capturing solar wind particles to studying lunar quakes, each tool transformed explorers into cosmic detectives, uncovering the Moon's secrets one data point at a time. As we peel back the layers of these scientific marvels, we're reminded that space exploration isn't just about adventure—it's about the pursuit of knowledge, the thrill of discovery, and the timeless journey to understand our universe, one lunar insight at a time.

Chapter 15: Collecting Moonstones: Sample Collection and Storage

Picture yourself on the Moon's surface, bathed in the eerie glow of lunar sunlight, surrounded by a stark, barren landscape that stretches as far as you can see. It's July 20, 1969, and you're not just any explorer; you're Neil Armstrong and Buzz Aldrin of Apollo 11, tasked with the extraordinary mission of collecting moonstones—precious samples that would rewrite the history of space exploration. This chapter takes you deep into the fascinating world of collecting and storing lunar samples, revealing the intricate techniques and cutting-edge technology that made this possible.

The Lunar Sample Collection Process:

Precise Procedures: Collecting lunar samples wasn't a haphazard operation. It was a meticulously planned and choreographed process. Astronauts followed precise procedures to ensure that the samples they gathered were untouched by Earth's atmosphere and untainted by human contamination. They had specialised tools at their disposal, including scoops, tongs, and sample bags designed to endure the harsh lunar environment.

Core Drilling: One of the primary methods used for sample collection was core drilling. Astronauts inserted a drill bit into the lunar regolith, extracting cylindrical cores of rock and soil. These cores were carefully sealed in specially designed sample containers for safe transport back to Earth.

Surface Rocks: In addition to core drilling, astronauts gathered surface rocks and loose soil. They wielded specialised scoops and tongs to pick up these samples, placing them gingerly into sample bags.

Technology at the Core:

Sample Containers: The lunar samples were incredibly precious, and their protection was paramount. They were placed in specially designed containers that shielded them from contamination and extreme temperatures. These containers were then stowed in the Lunar Module's Sample Return Container (SRC).

Sample Return Container (SRC): Think of the SRC as a lunar treasure chest. It was an airtight, temperature-controlled compartment that safeguarded the lunar samples during their journey back to Earth. It was like a high-tech safe, ensuring that the samples remained unaltered and preserved.

Vacuum Sealing: Each lunar sample container was hermetically sealed to prevent any interaction with Earth's atmosphere. This vacuum sealing was crucial in keeping the lunar samples in their pristine state for scientific analysis.

Sample Storage:

Lunar Receiving Laboratory: Once safely back on Earth, the lunar samples made their way to the Lunar Receiving Laboratory (LRL) at NASA's Johnson Space Center in Houston, Texas. It was here that rigorous containment protocols were established to prevent any potential lunar contaminants from escaping into our delicate biosphere.

Sample Handling: Inside the LRL, scientists and technicians dressed in full-body "moon suits" and worked within sealed glove boxes to handle the lunar samples. These measures ensured the highest level of containment and protection.

Sample Cataloging: The lunar samples were treated with the utmost care and respect. Each specimen received a unique identification number, meticulously cataloged to track its origin and history. This detailed record-keeping allowed scientists to trace the journey of every sample.

Scientific Insights: The lunar samples, brought back from the Moon's desolate surface, were not just rocks and dust; they were keys to unlocking the mysteries of our solar system.

Time Capsules: Through various analyses, scientists determined that these lunar rocks were roughly 4.5 billion years old, making them as ancient as the Earth itself. These findings supported the theory that the Moon was formed through a colossal impact with Earth.

Volcanic Clues: Some lunar samples contained tiny glass beads, evidence of ancient volcanic eruptions on the Moon. This offered valuable insights into the Moon's geologic history and evolution.

Solar Wind Whispers: By studying lunar soil, scientists gleaned information about the composition of the solar wind. This not only expanded our understanding of the Sun's elemental makeup but also helped us appreciate the broader cosmic picture.

The Legacy

The intricate techniques and state-of-the-art technology used in collecting and storing lunar samples during the Apollo 11 mission set a gold standard for future lunar explorations. These lunar samples continue to be a source of fascination and discovery. They are more than just rocks; they are time capsules that offer glimpses into the birth and evolution of our solar system. The Apollo 11 lunar samples stand as a testament to human curiosity, ingenuity, and our unquenchable thirst for knowledge about the cosmos.

Part VIII: Ascending from the Moon

Chapter 16: Leaving the Moon: Lunar Module Ascent

The moment had come. After an awe-inspiring moonwalk that would forever echo through the annals of history, Neil Armstrong and Buzz Aldrin prepared to embark on a journey that was as perilous as it was exhilarating: leaving the lunar surface. This chapter takes you on a thrilling ride through the Lunar Module's ascent procedure, revealing the challenges, the precision, and the courage that marked their ascent from the Moon.

The Precarious Start

Exiting the Moon's surface was no casual task; it was a momentous liftoff akin to a spaceship's departure from Earth. Here's a detailed look at the intricate procedure:

1. Pre-Ascent Checks: Before attempting the daring ascent, Armstrong and Aldrin conducted meticulous checks to ensure that their Lunar Module (LM), affectionately known as "Eagle," was primed and ready for action. These checks encompassed every aspect of the spacecraft's systems, from the engine's readiness to maintaining a seamless line of communication with Michael Collins in the orbiting

Command Module.

2. Ignition of Destiny: The cornerstone of their ascent lay in the ascent engine, a powerhouse nestled in the LM's lower section. The critical task of igniting this engine fell to Armstrong. The moment he fired it up, a surge of propulsive force would begin lifting the LM towards the Moon's orbit.

3. Precision Ascent: The lunar ascent demanded pinpoint precision. Any deviation from the meticulously calculated trajectory could spell disaster, leaving the astronauts stranded on the Moon. Armstrong, with his nerves of steel, manually piloted the LM, tracking the programmed ascent trajectory with unwavering focus.

4. Battling the Challenges:
- Limited Visibility: As the LM soared into the lunar sky, Armstrong and Aldrin were confronted with limited visibility. The LM's windows were not positioned to provide a panoramic view of the ascent. Instead, Armstrong had to rely on instruments and continuous communication with mission control to navigate this precarious journey accurately.

-Single Chance for Liftoff: Unlike Earth launches where you can adjust course if things go awry, on the Moon, there was no room for error. The LM's ascent engine had to ignite, propel them skyward, and achieve lunar orbit on the very first attempt. There were no second chances in this unforgiving environment.

-Engine Shutdown: The ascent engine burned for roughly seven and a half minutes, propelling the LM to lunar orbit. The shutdown sequence was executed with laser-like precision, ensuring that the LM and the orbiting Command Module could rendezvous harmoniously in space.

5. Rendezvous and Docking: The final stage of their departure was the dance of rendezvous and docking with the orbiting Command Module, where Michael Collins patiently awaited their return. This was a complex ballet of two spacecraft aligning themselves perfectly in the vastness of space, culminating in a delicate, yet essential, connection.

6. Homeward Bound: With the astronauts safely reunited aboard the Command Module, the trio embarked on their journey back to Earth, leaving the Moon behind. The LM, having served its monumental purpose, was no longer needed and was jettisoned, set on a trajectory that would ultimately lead it to impact the lunar surface.

The Reflection

Leaving the Moon was a pivotal moment, a poignant transition from the unearthly lunar landscape to the familiar embrace of Earth's orbit. It was the end of an odyssey that had captivated the world, an odyssey that had proven the indomitable spirit of human exploration. Departing the Moon was a testament to meticulous planning, engineering brilliance, and the unwavering resolve of astronauts who dared to reach for the stars. It marked the conclusion of one extraordinary chapter and the beginning of an enduring legacy.

Part IX: Journey Back Home

Chapter 17: Homeward Bound: Trans-Earth Injection and Return Trajectory

Hello, fellow cosmic adventurers! Prepare to be awed as we venture into the realm of celestial navigation, where the intricacies of space meet the precision of engineering. In this chapter, we're about to unravel the sophisticated technology and intricate calculations that guided Apollo 11's triumphant return journey from the Moon to Earth—a journey that exemplifies the marvels of human ingenuity.

Navigating the Void: Trans-Earth Injection's Delicate Art

Imagine the challenge of steering a spacecraft back to Earth from the Moon's distant shores. Trans-Earth injection was the moment when the course was set—a delicate ballet of thrust and gravity. Precision was the watchword. With engines ignited at just the right moment, Apollo 11's trajectory was gently tweaked, aiming for an intersection with Earth's path, millions of miles away.

Lunar Orbits and Gravitational Slingshots

Visualise the spacecraft circling the Moon, its engines poised for the trans-Earth injection burn. The Moon's gravity became a partner in this cosmic dance, a partner that would provide the energy needed to escape lunar orbit. This "slingshot effect" allowed Apollo 11 to borrow a bit of the Moon's energy, propelling it on its homeward journey.

Stitching the Stars: The Return Trajectory

Picture the spacecraft hurtling through space, stitching together the stars like cosmic constellations. The return trajectory wasn't a straight line; it was a complex arc that had to account for Earth's orbit, the Moon's gravitational pull, and the intricate dance of celestial bodies. Calculations guided the spacecraft's trajectory, ensuring it approached Earth at the right angle and speed.

Fiery Reentry: Earth's Warm Embrace

Envision the spacecraft blazing through Earth's atmosphere, flames flickering around its heat shield. The return trajectory had to be carefully crafted to ensure a controlled reentry. The angle had to be just right—too steep, and the heat generated could be catastrophic; too shallow, and the spacecraft could skip off the atmosphere like a stone on water. The heat shield, a technological marvel, protected the astronauts within from the scorching reentry.

Safe Splashdown: Earthly Reunion

Imagine the capsule descending gently under parachutes, the astronauts returning to their home planet with the Moon's secrets in tow. The return trajectory brought them to a precise splashdown point, a triumph of celestial navigation. Their return marked the successful execution of a meticulously planned journey, a culmination of teamwork, innovation, and the unyielding spirit of exploration.

Guided by the Stars

The technology behind trans-Earth injection and return trajectory is a testament to humanity's ability to navigate the vast cosmic expanse. As we delve into these intricate processes, we're reminded that space exploration isn't just about reaching destinations; it's about the entire cosmic voyage, from launch to reentry. Every calculation, every thruster burn, every celestial nudge is a tribute to human curiosity and determination. The return trajectory encapsulates the spirit of exploration—a journey guided by the stars, fuelled by knowledge, and destined to bring explorers back home, marking not just the end of one journey, but the beginning of the next chapter in our unending quest for the cosmos.

Chapter 18: Reentry and Splashdown: The Apollo 11 Return Module's Technology

Hello, intrepid explorers of the cosmos! Get ready to embark on the heart-pounding conclusion of Apollo 11's legendary journey—the reentry and splashdown. In this chapter, we're poised to uncover the intricate tapestry of cutting-edge technology and ingenious engineering that transformed the return module into a cosmic lifeboat, skilfully guiding Neil Armstrong, Buzz Aldrin, and Michael Collins through the fiery descent and triumphant homecoming.

The Fiery Gauntlet: From Vacuum to Atmosphere
Picture hurtling through the dark expanse of space, Earth's atmosphere beckoning ahead like a fiery gateway. Reentry was the moment of truth, a blistering transition from vacuum to atmosphere that demanded technological prowess. The return module's heat shield was the unsung hero—a specially designed armour that absorbed and dissipated the intense heat generated by friction during reentry.

Calculating Angle of Attack: Precision Amidst the Flames

Imagine the spacecraft angling itself like a daredevil, aiming to ride the fine line between too steep and too shallow. The angle of reentry was a delicate dance, a balance between speed and heat resistance. A miscalculation could lead to disaster. The spacecraft's trajectory was a symphony of calculations, ensuring that it would survive the inferno unscathed.

The Heat Shield: Engineering Wizardry

Visualise the heat shield glowing like a star as it absorbed the fiery assault. This marvel of engineering was a layered masterpiece, constructed from ablative materials that channeled the heat away from the spacecraft's delicate interior. With each layer burning away, the shield took the heat with it, leaving the astronauts inside comfortably cool amidst the cosmic inferno.

Parachutes and Graceful Descent: Returning to Earth

Picture the spacecraft descending under a canopy of parachutes, a serene ballet amidst the turbulence of reentry. The parachutes were the final act, slowing the return module's descent and ensuring a gentle splashdown. This stage required impeccable choreography—a symphony of parachute deployment, descent control, and ocean rendezvous.

A Watery Reunion: Apollo 11's Grand Finale

Envision the spacecraft gently bobbing on the ocean's surface, like a cosmic traveler returning home. The return module's flotation devices ensured that it remained buoyant while waiting for the recovery teams to arrive. This watery reunion marked the triumphant culmination of Apollo 11's odyssey—a testament to human achievement, knowledge, and courage.

Homeward Bound: Apollo 11's Return to Earth

As Apollo 11's astronauts bade farewell to the Moon, they knew that the most perilous part of their journey lay ahead—returning to Earth safely. Let's take an in-depth look at the meticulous steps and the passage of time as Apollo 11 made its triumphant return to our blue planet.

1. Lunar Orbit to Trans-Earth Injection: Timeframe - Approximately 75 hours after lunar liftoff.

-After leaving the lunar surface, the Lunar Module (LM) rendezvoused with the orbiting Command Module (CM) in lunar orbit.

- The LM's ascent stage, having fulfilled its purpose, was detached and intentionally crashed onto the

Moon's surface.

- Michael Collins, the Command Module Pilot, transferred from the CM into the Lunar Module to reunite with his fellow astronauts.

- The spacecraft was then precisely positioned in lunar orbit to execute the critical manoeuvre known as Trans-Earth Injection (TEI).

2. Trans-Earth Journey: Timeframe - About three days.

- With TEI completed, Apollo 11 embarked on its voyage back to Earth.

- The Command Module, under the guidance of Michael Collins, was reoriented for the homeward journey. Now, the spacecraft was influenced by Earth's gravitational pull and en route for reentry.

3. Course Corrections: Timeframe - Throughout the journey back.

- To guarantee a precise reentry, the spacecraft performed a series of course correction burns at calculated intervals. These mid-course adjustments were vital to ensure that the spacecraft arrived on target.

4. Entry into Earth's Atmosphere: Timeframe - Approximately 44 hours before splashdown.

- As Apollo 11 neared Earth, it plunged into the Earth's atmosphere. The immense speed and friction generated during reentry caused the spacecraft's heat shield to glow a fiery red. It was hurtling through space at speeds of roughly 25,000 miles per hour (40,000 kilometres per hour).

- The heat shield played a critical role, protecting the astronauts from the blistering heat generated during reentry. It slowly ablated away, dissipating the tremendous energy.

5. Parachute Deployment: Timeframe - A few minutes after entry.

- Once through the most intense phase of reentry, the Command Module initiated the deployment of a series of parachutes to decelerate its descent.
- Initially, a small pilot chute was deployed to extract the main parachutes. These colossal canopies further slowed the spacecraft's descent.

6. Splashdown: Timeframe - Approximately eight days, three hours, and 18 minutes after liftoff.

- Apollo 11's awe-inspiring journey culminated in a breathtaking splashdown in the vast expanse of the Pacific Ocean, approximately 13 miles (21 kilometres) from the recovery ship, the USS Hornet.
- Helicopters and recovery boats rapidly converged on the gently bobbing Command Module, successfully retrieving the astronauts and their invaluable lunar samples.

7. Quarantine: Timeframe - Following recovery.

- In a precautionary measure, the astronauts were placed in quarantine aboard the USS Hornet. This was done to ensure that no potentially hazardous lunar microorganisms had made the journey back to Earth.

- After a period of quarantine, it was determined that there were no biological threats, and the triumphant astronauts were allowed to step out and greet a world that had been riveted by their historic mission.

- The incredible journey of Apollo 11, from the Moon's surface to a triumphant splashdown in the Pacific Ocean, was a testament to human innovation, courage, and cooperation. It marked not only a giant leap for mankind but also a safe return home from the distant lunar landscape. The story of Apollo 11 will forever remain a shining example of what humanity can achieve when we set our sights on the stars.

The Epilogue of a Cosmic Journey

The reentry and splashdown of Apollo 11's return module weren't just feats of engineering; they were poetic moments that showcased humanity's relentless pursuit of exploration. As we delve into the intricate details of this cosmic ballet, we're reminded that space exploration isn't just about rockets and orbits; it's about conquering the challenges of reentry, navigating the storm of reintegration with our home planet, and emerging stronger and wiser. The return module's triumphant return, from the fiery embrace of reentry to the gentle touch of the ocean, is a reminder that the cosmos may be vast, but human ingenuity and courage are boundless—creating a legacy that reverberates through time and space, inspiring generations to dream beyond the stars.

Part X: Legacy and Future

Chapter 19: Reflections on Apollo 11: Technological Legacy and Future Endeavours

Hello, cosmic contemplators and visionaries! Prepare to embark on a thought-provoking journey as we gaze back at the awe-inspiring technological tapestry of Apollo 11 and its profound influence on the course of space exploration. In this chapter, we'll dive deep into the reflection pool and ponder the indelible legacy left by Neil Armstrong, Buzz Aldrin, and Michael Collins —a legacy that continues to guide our trajectory through the stars.

Apollo 11's Technological Odyssey: A Symphony of Human Ingenuity

Imagine the Earth collectively holding its breath as a solitary human footprint was etched onto the lunar surface—an image forever etched into history. Yet, this iconic moment was the culmination of an intricate symphony composed of technology, innovation, and human resilience. From the rumble of Saturn V's engines to the tranquility of the Moon's surface, every step of Apollo 11 was a testament to humanity's unwavering spirit to overcome challenges.

Legacy of Innovation: Planting Seeds for Cosmic Harvest

Visualise the Apollo 11 mission as a cosmic seed that sprouted into an era of space age advancements. The technology cultivated during this mission became the bedrock of future exploration. Lightweight materials, advanced guidance systems, and spacecraft design principles that were nurtured during Apollo 11 have blossomed into a flourishing garden of innovation, influencing how we approach modern space missions.

Pioneering Beyond the Moon: Lessons to Conquer Mars

Picture the wisdom garnered from Apollo 11's journey as the guiding star for humanity's next frontier—Mars. The lunar lessons, from grappling with inhospitable conditions to devising creative life support solutions, have found resonance in the quest for Mars exploration. The mission's successes and challenges serve as a treasure trove of insights, equipping us with the tools to boldly venture to the Red Planet.

Eyes on the Cosmos: A Continuation of the Journey

Envision the legacy of Apollo 11 as a celestial beacon, illuminating the path to the stars. The Moon landing wasn't humanity's final destination; it was a stepping stone that has propelled us further into the cosmic unknown. With advancements in propulsion, robotics, and the burgeoning field of space tourism, the torch ignited by Apollo 11 is being carried forward by a new generation, turning what was once a dream into a tangible, reachable reality.

A Tribute to Human Spirit: Eternal Flames of Inspiration

Reflect on how Apollo 11's legacy extends beyond technology—a lasting testament to the triumph of human spirit. The mission encapsulates the quintessential human traits of audacity, resilience, and boundless curiosity. It shows that the loftiest of dreams can be achieved through dedication and collaboration, igniting a spark within each of us to pursue the extraordinary.

Forging Ahead into the Unknown

In our reflections on Apollo 11's technological feats, we unearth a guiding compass that directs us toward the cosmic horizon. The legacy of the Moon landing isn't just a relic of the past; it's a blueprint for our cosmic future. The technology, the vision, and the spirit that propelled Apollo 11 have been woven into the fabric of our cosmic tapestry, shaping the way we explore, understand, and thrive within the universe. Just as Apollo 11 heralded the era of unprecedented achievement, our journey ahead promises fresh discoveries, unforeseen challenges, and stories of human brilliance yet to be written. The legacy of Apollo 11 invites us to embrace the unknown, for within its legacy lies the unwavering belief that the cosmos is our playground, beckoning us to dance among the stars.

END.

www.ingramcontent.com/pod-product-compliance
Lightning Source LLC
LaVergne TN
LVHW051707050326
832903LV00032B/4066